Boxer and the Fish

Written by Monica Hughes

Illustrated by Ann Ruozhu Sun

OXFORD
UNIVERSITY PRESS

Boxer was a big dog.

Boxer ran into town to look for food.

In a shop was ...

... a big fish!
Yum-yum! Dinner for me!

Boxer took the fish and ran off.

He ran down the road.

Boxer ran into the park.

In the park was a deep pool.

Boxer took a good look. In
the deep pool was ...

... a dog!

Yum-yum, a bigger fish for my dinner. I am going to get it!

The fish fell in the pool.

No! My fish!

Boxer was sad.

Retell the story

Once upon a time...

The end.